In loving memory of

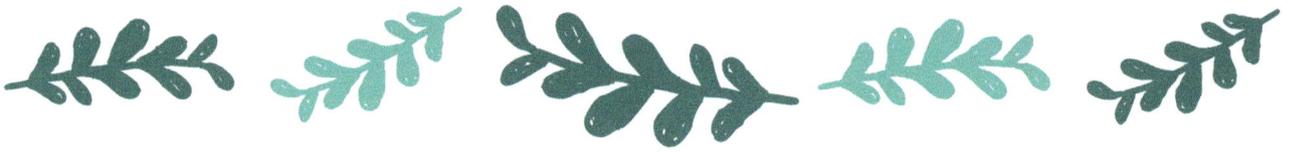

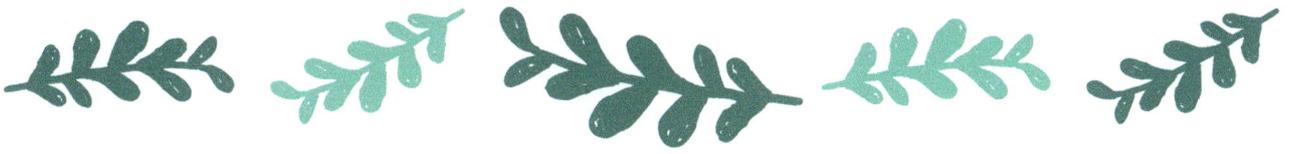

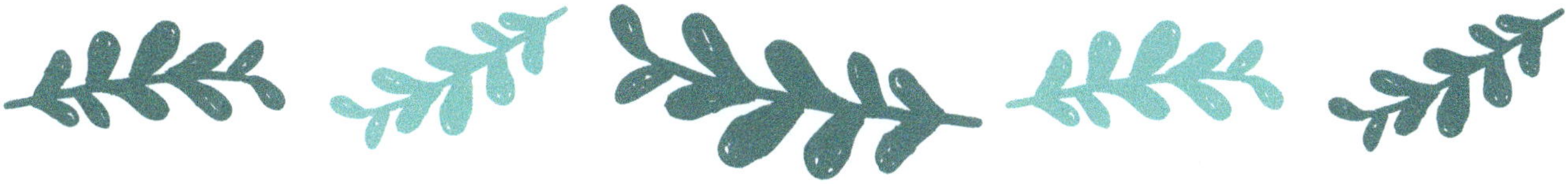

www.ingramcontent.com/pod-product-compliance
Lightning Source LLC
Chambersburg PA
CBHW041606260326
41914CB00012B/1403
9781912817733